Plan a Great Wedding in 3 Months or Less

Everything You Need for a Bride on a Tight Schedule

JUDY ALLEN

SOURCEBOOKS CASABLANCA™
AN IMPRINT OF SOURCEBOOKS, INC.®
NAPERVILLE, ILLINOIS

Published by Sourcebooks, Inc.
P.O. Box 4410, Naperville, Illinois 60567-4410
(630) 961-3900
FAX: (630) 961-2168
www.sourcebooks.com

Library of Congress Cataloging-in-Publication Data

Allen, Judy
Plan a great wedding in three months or less / Judy Allen.
p. cm.
ISBN 978-1-4022-0905-5
ISBN 1-4022-0905-3 (alk. paper)
1. Weddings—Planning. I. Title.
HQ745.A347 2005
395.2'2—dc22

2005021828

Printed and bound in China
LEO 10 9 8 7 6 5 4 3 2 1

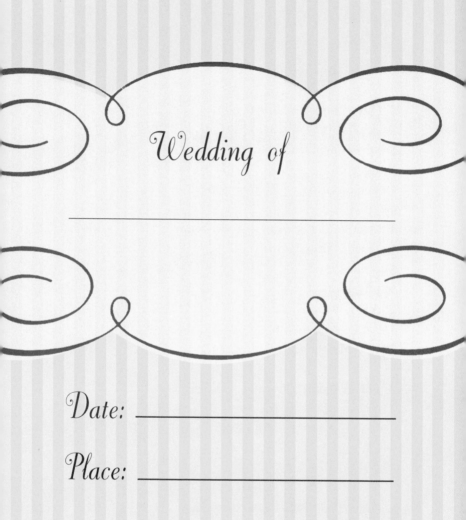

Wedding of

_____

Date: _____

Place: _____

Contents

How to Use Your Wedding Planner

∼

This planner is designed to show you the simplest, easiest way to create the wedding of your dreams with a quick turn-around. It will help you focus on what you need to do and when, provide you with creative wedding ceremony and reception site alternatives to consider (should you encounter limited availability), and show you how to stay on top of your wedding budget and follow your vision so that you can send out your wedding invitations in a timely manner and get on with planning the most exciting event of your life!

No matter the timeline of your engagement, all couples move through the exact same planning steps to produce the wedding of their dreams, so don't let the naysayers hold you back! These steps are relevant whether you are marrying locally, out of state, or out of the country. The critical wedding planning steps that professional planners follow—and you will employ—to produce a wedding day that will live up to your dreams are:

- Visualization: wedding day dreams
- Decision making: what matters most
- Choosing the perfect wedding and reception site
- Securing suppliers that will work for you
- Organizing wedding day timelines and wedding day flow

Keep in mind that this book is to be used as a guideline to break up tasks easily and efficiently. However, the more that can be done ahead of time will be beneficial to both your wedding and your peace of mind. Each venue and supplier has its own requirements, terms, and conditions and it might not follow the timeline provided here. Please keep that in mind as you plan your big day!

This planner will guide you through these steps— breaking them down into each of the twelve weeks you have to plan your big day and providing in-depth detail and essential worksheets. In each chapter, you will be given a list of objectives and the order in which they need to be done to accelerate the wedding planning process so you can spend your time concentrating on the things that matter most to you. You will be able to weigh your options quickly and determine where you most need to concentrate your energies. So relax, take a moment to get centered, and let's begin!

WEEK ONE:
Congratulations!

$\mathcal{C}$ongratulations on your upcoming nuptials! With the help of this planner, you'll be going from engaged to married in under twelve weeks. While the reasons couples decide to move quickly may vary, what you need to do to make your wedding day special doesn't.

The first step is for you to establish a vision of your wedding day so that you can get the necessary paperwork and phone calls in motion as soon as possible.

Basic Timing Considerations

1. What date have you selected?

_____

If you are selecting a date over a long weekend, be aware that you may have to pay extra for a reception site and staff wages. Additionally, the short notice for a holiday weekend may have an impact on your guest list RSVPs.

2. Your wedding season:

_____

This will influence the style and color of your dress and wedding party attire, as well as whether or not an outdoor ceremony or reception is possible.

3. Time of Day:

You may find that other weddings either precede or follow your celebration. You will need to arrange your festivities so that your guests will not arrive during another wedding or linger too long when another wedding follows yours.

Destination Weddings

You must determine immediately whether or not you will be having a destination wedding. A growing number of engaged couples look to combine their wedding with their honeymoon or jet off to an enticing location to elope. It can conceivably cost less to get married in this manner than to hold a full-scale wedding ceremony and reception, and if you have budget concerns, this may be an option worth pursuing.

If you do choose a destination wedding, it is likely that some of your loved ones will be unable to attend on such short notice. Also, you need to be sensitive to their financial situations, since it is costly to attend a destination wedding. However, if you decide to go ahead with this sort of wedding, it is possible to stream video footage of the ceremony live over the Internet.

Legal and Timing Considerations

If you decide on a destination wedding, there may be some legal issues that arise. Often, you will need certain documents (e.g., passports, translated documents, and travel permits) that may take several weeks to process. Some locations will also require you to obtain temporary residency or blood tests. Once you have decided to go away for your wedding or honeymoon, you will need to make these arrangements as soon as possible.

Budget

As you begin to envision your special day, you will want to consider any budget restrictions you may have. The Budget Planning Guide on page 77 will help you estimate what the total cost of your wedding will be.

Here are a few major components to keep in mind:

Wedding site

Reception site

Catering

Photography/Video

Wedding party attire

Floral arrangements

Music and entertainment

Determining What Matters Most

It is important for both of you to take the time to write down what matters most to you as you plan your special day. Once you have a clear vision of how you would like your wedding day to unfold, write down your preferences on the Wedding Vision Questionnaire on page 63. It's important to prioritize up front in order to avoid wasting time when problems or limitations arise. Additionally, having a strong, clear vision with a set budget and known priorities will carry you through every decision you have to make about your wedding day and related events. Let the tone of your wedding and your budget serve as your guide.

If you complete the preplanning process detailed in week one, begin working on the highest priority for week two: securing venues.

WEEK TWO:

Your Location &
Your Team

*N*ow that the two of you have decided exactly what you want, it is time to begin the decision-making process. During the second week of planning, you will need to make some quick decisions regarding your wedding so that you may begin to make the necessary phone calls.

Reserving Your Venues

You will need to reserve your ceremony and reception sites immediately. If your religious preferences allow it, you may want to find a reception facility where you can have your ceremony on the premises. If you decide to marry in a house of worship, you will need to determine what the requirements are if you and your fiancé are of different faiths. You will need to factor in the time that any premarital counseling courses will take, whether you are of the same faith or not.

Some of the most traditional and popular sites are:
    Places of worship
    Hotels
    Wedding chapels and halls
    Private homes and cottages
    Private indoor and outdoor spaces

As you call and visit venues, keep your budget and your vision in mind. Don't forgo unusual locales; often they make for the most memorable weddings.

Unusual locales include:

Local vineyards/wineries

Parks

Tourist attractions

Art galleries

Restaurants

Suppliers

Your suppliers are the people who provide goods and services for your wedding. They include florists, entertainers, caterers, chauffeurs, and rental companies. It is crucial to choose your suppliers at this stage and book them as soon as possible. You can keep track of your suppliers' contact information on the Suppliers' Information Worksheet on page 80. The following checklist will help you to cover all your bases.

Wedding Suppliers

❑ Wedding ceremony site

❑ Reception site

❑ Transportation (limousine, shuttle bus, etc.)

❑ Florist and decorations

❑ Rentals (chairs, tables, etc.)

❑ Musicians and/or DJs

❑ Photographer and videographer

❑ Caterer (food and beverages)

❑ Bakery

❑ Hotels (guest accommodations, wedding night, etc.)

There are nearly endless options for each supplier on your list. Don't be afraid to go off the beaten path to find creative solutions to scheduling and budget problems. Find a venue that also offers supplies (such as food, beverages, cake, cake cutting, and decorations) to save yourself some time. In this case, having a short schedule can work for you! Sought-after locations that have been reserved months in advance can open up as plans change. Don't let the short planning schedule keep you from calling your dream location or suppliers! Often, sites work with suppliers regularly and a reception site can offer a list of preferred vendors, including photographers, bakers, and entertainment.

Your suppliers will need information gleaned from your wedding vision, such as the number of guests, style, etc., in order to come on board in such a short time frame.

Photography

Memories of the day are enhanced by great photographs. There are many types of photographers to choose from and each has his or her own style—from traditional to photojournalistic. Knowing what you want and expressing your expectations to the potential photographer will help to ensure you get the most out of your investment. Be sure to provide your photographer with a shot list so he or she knows exactly what you want at the end of the day. Be sure to let your photographer know if any of your venues have regulations relating to flash photography or photography in general. Above all, find someone you can work with that has a style you admire.

Flowers

More than any other visual detail of your wedding, your guests will remember the flowers you select for both your wedding party and to decorate the venues. You will need to decide if you want floral garlands adorning the wedding party table, potted arrangements, vases, loose petals, etc. You will also need to decide if you plan to use real or silk flowers or something else entirely!

Ceremony Flowers

Flowers will help to make your ceremony bright, colorful, and unforgettable. Many religious establishments require real flowers at their altars. Keep this in mind as you plan your arrangements—if you are using silk flowers for your venues, you will need to find a florist to provide altar flowers for your ceremony. You will also need to arrange for pew bows or other adornments. Also, be sure to ask if your ceremony venue provides an aisle runner, or if you will need to provide your own.

Ceremony Floral Options Checklist

❏ Potted arrangements
❏ Floral vases
❏ Floral garlands
❏ Topiaries
❏ Hanging arrangements
❏ Floral archways

Reception Flowers

The right flowers will add elegance and vibrancy to your reception. Guests will feel as if they are in a wonderland if they are surrounded by fresh, fragrant blooms and dazzling arrangements. Some reception halls provide their own arrangements for buffet tables and head tables.

Reception Floral Checklist

- ❏ Potted arrangements
- ❏ Floral archways
- ❏ Vases/Topiaries
- ❏ Garlands
- ❏ Floral centerpieces
- ❏ Hanging arrangements
- ❏ Loose petals

Wedding Party Flowers

Your wedding party will also be decorated with beautiful floral arrangements. The following checklist will help you to cover all your bases for wedding party florals.

Wedding Party Floral Checklist

Bride

- ❏ Bouquet
- ❏ Floral headpiece
- ❏ Throwing bouquet
- ❏ Going away corsage/wristlet
- ❏ Honor attendant bouquet/boutonniere

- ❏ Attendants' bouquets/boutonnieres
- ❏ Flower girl petals

Groom
- ❏ Boutonniere
- ❏ Best man's boutonniere
- ❏ Groomsmens'/ushers' boutonnieres
- ❏ Ring bearer boutonniere
- ❏ Corsages and/or tussy mussies
  (mother of bride/groom, grandmothers, etc.)
- ❏ Boutonnieres
  (father of bride/groom, grandfathers, etc.)
- ❏ Wedding officiant

Legal Documents

If you have not done so already, you must apply immediately for any travel documentation you will need for your wedding or honeymoon. You should also contact your town hall to determine what documents are necessary to obtain a marriage license. Some states also require a simple blood test, which you should schedule as soon as possible. You can keep track of these requirements on the License and Legalities worksheet on page 75.

Legal Documents Checklist

- ❏ Passport and/or travel documents
- ❏ Certificate of death or divorce (if previously married)
- ❏ Blood test results, if required
- ❏ Social Security card
- ❏ Birth certificate

The Honeymoon

Now is the time to book your honeymoon accommodations. Often, you can book hotel rooms and airline tickets online, which may eliminate a lot of time spent on the phone. Making your reservations online also allows you to compare prices quickly and see photographs of both the exterior and interior of your hotel. Try using a full-service provider such as *distinctivehoneymoons.com,* as they supply advice and experience as well as offer a destination wedding and honeymoon bridal registry as a special gift option for your family and friends. Additionally, don't forget that travel agents have often been to the places they book so take advantage of their expertise; you don't want to risk your honeymoon being spoiled due to a desire to save what may be a small amount of money. Comparison shopping and personal testimonies are always important when making travel arrangements.

WEEK THREE:

Family, Friends, & Loved Ones

*C*ongratulations! You have already contacted all of the venues and suppliers for your big day. Now you will need to establish a working guest list and order your invitations, as well as make arrangements for your rehearsal dinner.

The Guest List

This may be the most time-consuming aspect of the planning process for you, so be sure to set enough time aside for this step with your fiancé. It is important to have an approximate head count at this stage, as you may be signing contracts and establishing an estimate with your suppliers. You will also need to consider whether or not your venues have limited capacity— if so, you will need to limit your list. Also, don't forget to invite your officiant to the reception—wedding etiquette experts agree that this is a must! See the Guest List Worksheet on page 81 to keep track of whom you plan to invite.

Guest List Totals

Bride's Family _____

Groom's Family _____

Wedding Party _____

Total _____

Choosing Your Wedding Party

You will avoid a lot of hurt feelings if you choose your attendants early on, so now is the time to decide on your wedding party. Typically, there is one usher per fifty guests. You may also want to select a best man and an honor attendant, as well as a ring bearer and a flower girl. Log the contact information of your wedding party in the Wedding Party Contact Sheet on page 83.

The maid of honor usually organizes your bridal shower and any bachelorette celebrations. She also keeps track of gifts during the shower and helps you to maneuver in your dress on the wedding day. The best man often gives the wedding toast at the reception, picks up the tuxes, organizes the bachelor party, and is responsible for bringing the rings to the ceremony.

Invitations

Now that you've decided who to invite, you will need to order your invitations; because your time is limited, you must act quickly. You may opt to design your invitations on your home computer and then print them at a nearby office supply store. You can also order beautiful, professional invitations—though you may have to pay a fee for a rush order.

Often, brides select invitations based on the color scheme of their wedding. The following checklist will help you to decide what to include in the envelope:

Invitation Checklist

❏ Invitation envelope
❏ Lined
❏ Unlined
❏ Invitation text and style
❏ Formal
❏ Informal
❏ Reply card
❏ Stamped, addressed reply envelope
❏ Dinner card with meal selections
❏ Map/Directions

Note: You will want your RSVP date to be two weeks before the wedding or earlier, depending on the needs of your location or food and beverage suppliers. Some couples choose to have an online guestbook or tracker for RSVPs to save guests time and save themselves postage.

The Rehearsal

Now that you have chosen your wedding party, it is important to schedule a rehearsal with your officiant. If you are having your ceremony in a church or synagogue, you may run into scheduling trouble if you wait too long to block off rehearsal time.

A rehearsal dinner can range from a casual backyard barbecue to a fancy dinner at a restaurant. If you decide to hold your rehearsal dinner at a restaurant, or would like to cater a meal at home, you will need to make these arrangements at this stage.

WEEK FOUR:
The Bride Goes Shopping

$\mathcal{T}$ake a deep breath and relax. Now that you have established your guest list, ordered the invitations, selected your bridal party, and booked your rehearsal, you are well on your way. Now, for the fun part: selecting a dress and registering for gifts.

The Wedding Dress

Many women have dreamed of their wedding dress since they were little girls. You probably have some idea of what style you want based on your body type and preferences. However, you will need to start trying dresses on and making a final decision so that your seamstress will have ample time to make the first round of alterations.

Wedding Dress Checklist

❑ Color _____

❑ Cut _____

❑ Train?

       Yes___

       No___

❑ Veil?

       Yes___

       No___

❑ Crinoline slip/special undergarments needed?

       Yes___

       No___

❑ Cost $ _____

Consult with family and friends and pick the dress that makes you feel beautiful but reasonably comfortable—it's going to be a long day in that dress and those shoes! Once you have selected the perfect dress, buy any special under-garments or slips you will need so that your measurements are accurate. You will also need to buy your shoes before your first fitting so that the dress is tailored properly. Once you have selected your dress, start thinking about any jewelry or accessories you would like to wear.

If you order a dress online, stick to the sizing charts. Don't plan to lose weight by the wedding and order a size to small. Remember: a large dress can always be made smaller, but a small dress never grows to fit!

Bridesmaids' Dresses

You will also need to select your bridesmaids' dresses at this point. Select a color (or colors) that complements your venue, the season, and your taste. You may also want to consider how their dresses will look next to yours in photos. Bring your bridesmaids with you when you try on wedding gowns, as they will be able to try on gowns themselves. No matter where you order the dresses, choose a retailer that offers on-site alterations to save a lot of time and hassle down the road.

Be sensitive to the body types and preferences of your bridesmaids. We have all heard nightmarish stories about bridesmaids' gowns, and you want your most beloved friends and family to feel comfortable. Many bridal stores

offer two-piece ensembles that allow bridesmaids to select a top that best complements their body type and style preferences.

Gift Registries

Even if you and your fiancé live together, there are probably household items you need or want to upgrade. Even if you know that your family will likely give you cash, register for gifts. A "green only" notation on invitations is tacky. Also, a registry will help to eliminate duplicate items, sparing you a tedious return and exchange process.

To save time, you may want to register online for gifts. Stores like Target and Linens 'n Things offer online registries, which will also save your guests a lot of time. Most stores will send registry cards printed with your name to include in shower invitations. Never include registry cards in wedding invitations.

Here are some basic gift registry ideas:
  Small kitchen appliances
      (coffee makers, blenders, toasters, etc.)
  Kitchen utensils/accessories
  Table linens (napkins, placemats, etc.)
  Flatware
  Dishes, glassware, and china
  Small household appliances
      (clocks, vacuum cleaners, etc.)
  Bathroom accessories
      (soap dishes, wastebaskets, etc.)
  Bath towels, hand towels, and washcloths
  Bed sheets, comforters, curtains, and quilts
  Cookbooks

Unconventional registries, such as for your honeymoon or stock portfolio are also growing in popularity.

WEEK FIVE:
With This Ring

*D*uring your fifth week of planning, you'll need to shop for a flower girl dress and choose wedding bands with your husband-to-be. By this time, you have chosen your dress and will be able to find a flower girl gown that complements yours.

The Flower Girl Gown

Many brides select flower girl dresses that mimic their own gowns; however, this isn't necessary. Most bridal retailers offer a wide selection of flower girl dresses that will complement most styles and colors. If possible, be sure to take the flower girl's mother along with you for the fitting so that she will feel as comfortable as possible as she tries on gowns. To save time, buy a flower girl basket and tiara (if necessary) at the store. You can also buy these items inexpensively at discount retailers or the wedding section of a local crafts store.

The Wedding Bands

You also need to select your wedding bands during week five, just in case you need to make special sizing or custom arrangements. This is especially important if you have an odd-shaped engagement ring that will require a custom-designed band, or if you plan to engrave your rings.

Wedding Band Decisions

❏ Custom-made?

  Yes____

  No____

❏ Metal:

  Gold____

  Silver____

  Platinum____

  Other____

❏ Engraved?

  Yes____

  No____

❏ Style:

  Plain____

  With stones____

If you opt for simple rings, you can often find inexpensive plain gold bands in department stores. If yours is not an exact fit, you can take it to a ring-sizing booth at your local shopping mall or to a jeweler for resizing.

WEEK SIX:
In the Details

You are halfway to your wedding, and look at how much you have accomplished! Now, you will need to plan some of the aesthetics of your ceremony and reception.

Table Centerpieces

Aside from the flowers, the table centerpieces are generally the most important aesthetic element of your reception. Again, you must decide what centerpiece best fits your wedding vision. Centerpieces don't always have to be flowers. Today the options are endless and increasingly creative, from reinforcing a theme to making an unusual statement about the couple. However, no matter what you decide for your centerpiece arrangements, be sure to have glass shields surrounding any candles you use to prevent your flowers or other decorations from catching fire. Quality battery operated candles with variable flicker speeds are a viable option for venues that do not permit open flames, and they can be used again for home entertaining.

Personalized Elements

Now is the time to decide on personalized items and to place orders. Planning on having matchbooks, ribbon, or candies with your names and the date? Order those this week. Also, if you plan to have any handmade decorations or favors to assemble, get a jump on these as soon as possible.

Reception Favors

Most likely, your guests will be giving you generous gifts for your wedding. In return, it is customary to give your guests some sort of memento to commemorate your special day. You will also want to feature a guest book for them to write their congratulations.

Here are some ideas for wedding favors:
- Candles/candleholders
- Custom CDs with some of your favorite love songs
- Seeds or seedlings in pretty packaging
- Frames with a picture of the two of you inside
- Personalized candy bars, matchbooks, etc.
- Engraved champagne glasses
- Small boxes or bags that contain nuts, candy, or chocolates

Whatever you decide to give, be sure to order them now. Some craft stores sell candleholders and frames in bulk for just this purpose, which may be a particularly time-saving option for you.

WEEK SEVEN:
Music and Cake

By now, your wedding has begun to take shape. Now, you will need to meet with any entertainers or performers to select music for your ceremony and reception, order the wedding cake, and send your invitations.

Music Matters

The music that you select for your wedding will set the tone for the day. You will need to meet with your musicians (i.e., organist, band, D.J., etc.) to choose songs for your special day.

Ceremony Music

Selecting your ceremony music is often a simple matter of sitting down with your organist, harpist, or vocalist to select the perfect music for when you walk down the aisle. However, if you are selecting special songs that may not be in a musician's repertoire, you will need to find the sheet music. The following list will help you to track the various stages of the ceremony that will require music.

Ceremony Songs

Seating music

_____

Bridesmaids' march

_____

Processional

_____

Recessional

_____

Reception Music

The music that you choose for your reception will become one of your most treasured wedding memories. Meet with your DJ or band to select the following songs:

Reception Songs (yours may vary)

First dance

_____

Father of the bride

_____

Mother of the groom

_____

Bridal party dance

_____

Last dance

_____

Sending the Invitations

Now is the time to send your wedding invitations. You will want to address all of the envelopes in cursive or calligraphy. For your purposes, you may want to print them from your home computer.

When you prepare your invitations, be sure that all names and addresses are spelled correctly to ensure speedy delivery. Heart-shaped envelope seals and calligraphy are optional accoutrements that go in and out of fashion, but use of such things should be dictated, again, by your style and your budget.

Meeting with the Officiant

You will want to meet with your officiant at this point to finalize details of your ceremony. If you are marrying in a Catholic church, you will need to decide whether you want a simple ceremony or full mass. If you are including any special traditions in your wedding, establish them now so that you will be able to create your wedding program during the next planning week. You will also need to determine whether or not you will recite vows or write your own.

The Wedding Cake

Because you have such limited time, your best bet for a wedding cake is a local bakery. To save transportation costs, you may want to choose one as close to your reception venue as possible. Many bakeries offer beautiful cakes in a variety of flavor combinations and are usually more willing to accommodate short-notice requests than specialty cake designers. High-end grocers often offer exceptional value so don't be afraid to ask.

Here are some factors that you will need to consider when ordering your cake:

- Guest count
- Type of cake
- Frosting style and/or flavor
- Filling flavor
- Decorative topper or flowers
- Detailing
- Number of tiers

WEEK EIGHT:

Looking Beautiful

$\mathcal{N}$ ow that you are in your eighth week of planning, you will want to finalize your bridal accessories and cosmetic needs. Your groom will need to have his first round of tux fittings with his groomsmen and ring bearer. You will also create your wedding programs.

Bridal Accessories

At this stage, you should purchase any accessories necessary to complete your bridal ensemble. You will want them to complement your dress without outshining it, so select elegant, dainty pieces with just the right amount of sparkle. This checklist will help you to determine what you want to include.

Accessories Checklist

❏ Earrings
❏ Necklace/choker
❏ Bracelet
❏ Tiara/hair accessories
❏ Purse
❏ Gloves
❏ Garter

Hair and Makeup

Make your appointment now for your wedding day hair and makeup, as well as a manicure and pedicure a few days before the wedding if necessary. If at all possible, choose a salon that does both hair and makeup on the premises. Not only will this simplify your planning, but it will also save you a lot of time on your wedding day. You will also want to schedule a test run for yourself (about a week before the wedding) so that you know exactly how you will look on your wedding day.

There are many possible hairstyles for your wedding day, but the standards are:

The curled up do
The French twist
The half-up do
Down and sleek
Down and curled

There are many variations on these themes, including decorative hair weaving, rhinestone accessories, twists, etc. Before you visit your hairdresser for your test run, look at some bridal magazines or websites so that you have an idea as to what you want. Your hairdresser can help you make a final decision based on your facial structure and your veil.

Wedding Programs

Now that you have finalized your ceremony music, you have all the necessary pieces to create a wedding program. A wedding program serves double duty for guests: it maps out the ceremony for guests, and it becomes a keepsake for them. There are websites that will help you to create programs from your home computer, as well as companies who will print them for you. Check prices and styles and consider your options. If you opt to print them yourself, print them this week and store them someplace safe.

WEEK NINE:

Planning for Your Honeymoon

*C*ongratulate yourself! Everything has been booked, everyone has been invited, and all of your remaining tasks have already been set in motion. Now, you will need to do some shopping, both for yourself and your bridal party, as well as enjoy your bridal shower!

The Bridal Shower

Your bridal shower is a wonderful opportunity to spend time with your favorite female friends and relatives (unless you have a coed Jack-and-Jill shower) before the wedding. You will also receive many gifts to help you begin your new life. Odds are, your maid of honor orchestrated this event, so all you need to do is sit back and enjoy the party.

Opening gifts in front of so many guests can be overwhelming, but just remember to smile and be gracious. One of your bridesmaids should keep a list of guests and the gifts they bring so that you have a blueprint for your thank-you notes later. Be sure to have a safe place for any cash or gift cards that might get lost in the shuffle.

Bridal Party Gifts

It is customary for a bride to give some sort of gift to her bridesmaids and flower girl as a token of her love and appreciation.

Here are some ideas for your bridesmaids' gifts:

Jewelry

Handbags

Engraved compact or keychain

Jewelry boxes

Photo album

You can give a similar gift to your flower girl, but it is also appropriate to buy her a toy or special doll that she can treasure forever.

Rehearsal and Honeymoon Attire

If you haven't shopped for your rehearsal outfit or honeymoon clothing yet, now is the time to do so.

Rehearsal Outfit

Your rehearsal outfit will depend on how casual your dinner will be; however, as a general rule, jeans and T-shirts are not acceptable for this occasion. Often, brides choose a simple sleeveless or strapless dress, or a dressy skirt and top. Your outfit will depend on the season, but avoid bulky sweaters or pants.

The groom should wear a button-down shirt and tie. For a formal rehearsal dinner, he should wear a suit. For a more informal affair, he can wear dressy khakis instead of a suit.

Going-Away Outfit

Many brides opt to dance their last reception dance in a white "going-away" outfit. This outfit can be fairly casual, but should be white in honor of the occasion. A white skirt or dress pants are appropriate with a dressy blazer, top, or blouse.

Honeymoon Clothing

You will need to buy a variety of outfits for your honeymoon. It is a good idea to check the weather patterns for your destination and pack clothing for a variety of weather scenarios.

Honeymoon Attire Checklist

❑ Lingerie
❑ Sweater or cardigan (for chilly nights)
❑ Dressy outfit/dress (for fancy dinners)
❑ Beach cover-up
❑ Flip-flops/sandals
❑ Walking shoes/sneakers
❑ Jacket/coat/mittens
  (for colder honeymoon locales)
❑ Sunglasses/visor
❑ Swimsuits

WEEK TEN:

Don't Forget the Marriage License!

*B*elieve it or not, you will get your marriage license this week! You will also create a seating chart and place cards for your reception guests, have your final fittings, and write the thank-you cards for your shower gifts.

The Marriage License

Typically, couples apply for their marriage licenses a week or two before the wedding. Early in the planning process, you determined what was required to obtain the license, so you should have all the necessary documents by now. If there is no waiting period in your state, you should get your marriage license at this point.

Here is a checklist of things you may need to bring when you apply for your certificate, depending on your state:

Needed for License
❏ Birth certificate
❏ Social security card/visa
❏ Photo ID
❏ Immunization records
❏ Blood test results
❏ Proof of death, divorce, or annulment
❏ Cash or a check (to pay fee)

The Seating Chart

Aside from composing the guest list itself, this is the trickiest aspect of the wedding planning process. In some cases, you may choose an open seating system, but this will not be possible if you are having a sit-down dinner and guests have ordered entrées in advance.

You are not going to please all of your guests, no matter how much care and attention you give to your seating chart. The important thing is that your seating chart groups people who know one another, or people in a similar age group who are sure to have fun together.

The Final Guest Seating Chart on page 87 will help you to decide who will sit where.

Final Fittings

Now is the time to make any final alterations to your dresses and tuxes. The bridal party will meet with the seamstress at this point for any last-minute alterations before the wedding gown is steamed. The same applies for the groom and his party. Arrange for one of your attendants to pick these items up the day before the wedding.

Shower Gift Thank-You Notes

Now is also the time to send out your shower gift thank-you notes. Ideally, your guests will receive them before the wedding. Be sure to be personal—your guests will revel in knowing that their gift and presence brought you joy. Use the gift list that your maid of honor created at the shower to specify what you're thankful for in each card.

WEEK ELEVEN:
Coming into the
Home Stretch

*T*hings are really getting down to the wire now, but fear not! Everything that you need to do at this point has been arranged, and you simply need to show up.

Hair and Makeup Test Run

When you show up for the salon test run, you should already know exactly what you want your hair to look like. Your hairdresser will review your favorite photos and begin to craft a hairstyle that will complement your dress and withstand the hours of dancing you will be doing at your reception.

If you have also arranged to have your makeup done at the salon, a cosmetician will ask you questions about your color scheme and find the best look for you based on your skin tone. Don't be afraid to speak up if the lipstick is too dark or your eyeliner seems too severe.

Final Review with Vendors

- Call the bakery and venues with your final head count so that your cake, food, and beverage supplies will be as close to exact as possible, if you haven't already. Each vendor likely has their own timeline for contractual purposes. It's important to honor these dates.
- Follow-up with all vendors that have not already confirmed final details with you in writing.

Pick Up Your Rings

If you've had your rings sized, engraved, or custom-made, you will need to pick them up to be certain that your ring fits and is engraved correctly. Entrust the best man with this precious jewelry—he will bring it to the ceremony on your wedding day for the ring bearer.

The Bachelor/Bachelorette Party

Odds are, your honor attendants have planned a special evening for each of you. This is a chance to unwind after your final week of planning and spend some time with your favorite people before the big day. A bachelorette or bachelor party can be any one of the following:

- A night at the casino
- An informal party at someone's house or apartment
- A special dinner out together
- Going to a club to dance and enjoy some cocktails

WEEK TWELVE:
The Big Day

*T*his is it! By the end of the week, you will be married and on your way to your honeymoon. We will break this final chapter into each of the seven days before your wedding.

Day One

- Shop for any toiletries that you will need for your honeymoon.
- Prepare a wedding day personal care/emergency supplies kit

Wedding Day Survival Kit

- ❑ Aspirin or other pain reliever
- ❑ Breath mints
- ❑ Chalk (to hide smudges on dress)
- ❑ Clear nail polish (for runs, etc.)
- ❑ Deodorant
- ❑ Energy bars
- ❑ Extra panty hose
- ❑ Feminine products
- ❑ Handkerchief
- ❑ Honeymoon documents and suitcases
- ❑ Keys
- ❑ Kleenex
- ❑ Lint roller
- ❑ Makeup for touchups
- ❑ Medication (upset stomach, decongestant, etc.)
- ❑ Nail polish for touchups and nail repair glue
- ❑ Safety pins
- ❑ Travel or steam iron

Day Two

- Now is a good time to get a quick, but important task done. You should prepare payment envelopes for each of the service providers you will need to pay on your wedding day. This checklist will help you keep track of people you may need to pay on the wedding day:

Payment Envelopes

- ❏ Officiant
- ❏ Organist/harpist/musicians
- ❏ Limousine driver
  (gratuity, if not included in bill)
- ❏ Photographer/Videographer
- ❏ Caterer
- ❏ Reception facility
- ❏ DJ/band
- ❏ Other providers

Entrust these envelopes to someone who will remember to pay all of the necessary people on the wedding day.

Day Three

- If necessary, pick up your marriage license from the town hall and keep it in a safe place. Arrange for someone to bring it to the rehearsal for the officiant to sign.
- Wrap favors and pack them into boxes.

Day Four

- If either of you is moving, fill out change-of-address forms at your post office. If you are changing your last name, wait until after the wedding to change information on your driver's license, insurance, monthly bills, bank accounts, Social Security, etc. Most of these companies will require a copy of your marriage license, which won't likely be available until a few weeks after the wedding.

Day Five

- Have your manicure and pedicure done. You may not have time for this on the day of your rehearsal or wedding.
- Pack for your honeymoon. Purchase anything you have forgotten, or go without! This will be your last opportunity to do any shopping.
- Confirm drop-off times with your florist.

Day Six

- Arrange for one of your attendants to pick up your dresses and tuxes.
- Drop off your centerpieces, guest book, and favors at the reception site for the staff to arrange.
- Drop off your cake topper at the bakery.

- **Your rehearsal:** Don't forget the marriage license! This is a chance for you to practice your vows and get used to standing at the altar in front of people. Your officiant will discuss with you how the ceremony will unfold and in what order things will happen.
- **Your rehearsal dinner:** This should be a relaxing, fun time for the two of you as you anticipate a day that has been three months in the making! This is also an appropriate time to hand out your bridal party gifts.

Day Seven: The Wedding

Congratulations! Your wedding day has finally arrived. Here are the things that you will need to do before, during, and after your ceremony.

Before the Ceremony

- *Eat breakfast!* No matter how nervous you are, you will only feel worse if your stomach is empty as you walk down the aisle.
- Go to the salon for hair and makeup. Be sure to wear a button-down shirt to avoid ruining your hairstyle. Don't forget your veil, tiara, or any other hair accessories you plan to use.
- If necessary, be sure that someone is picking up all of the wedding party flowers.
- Assemble any personal items you will need in your wedding purse, including cash, aspirin, breath mints, antacids, or feminine products. Also, arrange

for one of your family members to bring your going-away outfit to the reception.

- Touch up your nails if necessary.
- Get into your wedding gown, garter, and shoes. By now, the photographer will have probably arrived and begun to take pictures.
- When the limousine arrives, take a deep breath. *This is it!*

During the Ceremony

- Smile, smile, and smile. It's clinically proven to reserve any stage fright you may be feeling!

After the Ceremony

- Your photographer will want to take pictures of the newlyweds (you!), the wedding party, and the families.
- Get into the limousine to go to the reception!

The Reception

- Your band or D.J. are the choreographers of the event and will announce all of the special dances, cake cutting, bouquet toss, and last dance.
- Before your last dance, change into your going-away outfit if you have purchased one.
- Leave for your wedding night or honeymoon. *Bon voyage!*

Wedding Vision Questionnaire

Make two copies of this form—one for the bride, one for the groom.

Wedding Date

- During what time of year (season) do I visualize our wedding being held? _____
- How much wedding planning time will that give me? _____
- What day of the week do I want our wedding to take place on?

  _____
- What time of day do I prefer to be married at? _____
- Is there a special date that is significant to me that I want to be married on or any date that I want to avoid? _____
- Will the time of year, month, date, or time affect attendance of close family members and friends that I want to be with me on our special day? _____
- Where (location, not venue) will our wedding ceremony ideally take place? _____

  _____

Check any critical dates that may be taking place around your selected wedding date, such as major personal, family, or friend events (graduation, birth due date of a baby, special anniversary, birthday celebrations, national or religious holidays, or long weekends that could affect supplier delivery and guest attendance).

Bride's Family

- What immediate family members will be part of our wedding ceremony? _____

  _____

Wedding Vision Questionnaire

Groom's Family
- What immediate family members will be part of our wedding ceremony?
  _____
  _____

Wedding Party
- Who will be walking me/us down the aisle? _____
- How many people in total will be in our wedding party? _____
    - Maid/Matron of Honor _____
    - Bridal Attendants _____
    - Best Man _____
    - Groomsmen _____
- Will we be having a:
    - Flower Girl? _____
    - Ring Bearer? _____
    - Ushers? _____
- Will the members of the wedding party be invited to bring a guest?
  _____

Wedding Guests
- Do I prefer a large or small wedding? _____
- How many guests do I visualize attending? _____
- Will single guests be invited to bring a guest? _____
- What is the age range of the guests we will be inviting? _____
- Do I see children being invited to our wedding? _____
- Will any guests have any special needs, such as handicap accessibility? _____
- Will any of the guests have to come in from another town, state, or country? _____
- Will we be required to host or entertain out-of-town guests?_____

Wedding Vision Questionnaire

Invitations
- Am I open to invitation styles or do I have something particular in mind? _____

Wedding Ceremony
- Where do I see our wedding ceremony taking place and our vows being exchanged? _____
- Is the wedding ceremony taking place inside or outside? _____
- Do I see our wedding ceremony being a formal or informal event?

  _____
- What do I see the wedding party wearing? _____
- Where is the wedding ceremony location in relationship to where we live? _____

  _____
- Where is the wedding ceremony location in relationship to where our guests live? _____
- Will a bridal suite be required at the wedding ceremony location for the bride, groom, or any other members of the bridal party to dress in? _____

Wedding Ceremony Décor
- As the guests are arriving at the wedding ceremony, what do I envision they will see from the moment that they arrive until they are seated? _____
- How do I envision the wedding ceremony stage to look? _____

  _____
- What are my favorite flowers? _____

  _____
- What flowers hold special meaning for me? _____

  _____
- What flowers hold special meaning for us as a couple? _____

  _____
- What is my favorite color? _____
- What wedding color scheme am I initially drawn to? _____

  _____

Wedding Vision Questionnaire

Wedding Ceremony Music
- What do I imagine our wedding guests will be listening to while they wait for the bridal party to arrive? _____
- What type of music will be playing as the bridal procession begins? _____
- What song will signal the arrival of the bride? _____
- Will live musical performances be a part of our wedding processional or ceremony? _____

Wedding Ceremony Lighting
- What ambience does the lighting project? _____
_____
- What mood do I want the room to convey? _____
_____

Wedding Party Arrival
- How do I see the wedding party arriving at the ceremony? Will they be making their own way there, have drivers assigned to them, or arrive by limousine or some other transportation mode? _____
_____
- What transportation do I envision for the bride and the groom to the ceremony? _____
- Where will we be coming from (e.g., parents' home, friend's home, hotel, or other location) _____
- Who will be accompanying each of us? _____

Wedding Photographs at the Ceremony
- Will we be having professional wedding photographs, videos, or a live wedding webcast of our ceremony? _____
- Who will be taking wedding photographs or videos? _____

Wedding Vision Questionnaire

Wedding Vows

- What is of utmost importance to me to have in our wedding ceremony? _____
- Who do I see conducting the wedding ceremony? _____
- Do I see us exchanging traditional wedding vows, vows tailored to us, or vows written by us? _____
- Are there any special family, cultural, or religious traditions that would be very meaningful to me or to us to include? _____
  _____
- How do I see the wedding processional unfolding? _____
  _____
- How long do I see the wedding ceremony taking from beginning to end? _____
- After we are joined in matrimony and are exiting the wedding stage, what do I see taking place? _____
  _____
- What music will be played as we are introduced to our guests and walk back down the aisle as husband and wife? _____
  _____

Wedding Photographs Before or After the Ceremony

- Will I want family photographs taken before or after the ceremony?
  _____
- What backdrop will I want to see in my wedding photographs?
  _____
- How will the wedding party be transported to the photograph location and wedding reception?
  _____

Wedding Vision Questionnaire

Wedding Reception Venue

- Will I want the wedding ceremony and wedding reception to take place in the same location?_____
- If our reception is being held in a secondary location, will it present any transportation concerns for our guests? _____
- Where do I see our wedding reception taking place? _____
- What type of venue would best suit our wedding reception? _____
  _____
- Do I see the wedding reception taking place inside or outside? ____
  _____
- Do I see our wedding reception being a formal or informal event? ___
  _____

Wedding Reception Arrival

- Do I see the guests arriving at the venue in advance of the wedding party (e.g., while photographs are being taken)? _____
- What do I have in mind for the guests to do in the interim (e.g., will there be refreshments and entertainment)? _____
- Will we need a separate area in which to host the arrival and then move the guests into another room once the wedding party arrives? _____
  _____
- Will seating be required for any or all of the guests? _____
- Will we have a receiving line? _____
- How do I see our reception unfolding? _____
  _____
- How long do I see our reception going on? _____

Wedding Reception Room Requirements

- How do I see the room being laid out? _____
- Will it be a stand-up reception with scattered seating? _____
- Will it be a sit-down affair with table seating for all guests? _____
- If we are including dinner, will seating be open or will we having set seating and a seating chart? _____

Wedding Vision Questionnaire

- Will there be food stations or buffet setups or will food be passed or plated? _____
- Will there be bars set up in the room or will beverages be served by waitstaff? _____
- Where will the wedding party be seated? _____
- Where will the wedding cake be positioned? _____
- Will a stage be required for speeches, the musicians, DJ, or entertainment? _____
- Will there be dancing? _____
- Will there be any audiovisual requirements such as rear screen projection, plasma screens, etc., which need to be factored into the room size requirements? _____
  _____

Wedding Reception Décor

- As the guests are arriving at the wedding reception, what do I envision they will see as they arrive? _____
- What type of décor do I see in the room? _____
- How do I see the room being set? Table settings? Centerpieces? Flowers? Colors? What do I see in the room? _____
  _____

Wedding Reception Entertainment

- Will we have a DJ, live musicians, a dance band, or piped-in background music? _____
  _____
- What type of music will be played? _____
- What song do I see us dancing our first dance to? _____
- Who will be our MC? _____

Wedding Reception Lighting

- How do I see the room being lit? _____

Wedding Vision Questionnaire

Wedding Reception Audiovisual

- Will there be speeches or toasts? _____
- Will a podium or microphones be required? _____
- Will we have any audiovisual requirements? _____

Wedding Reception Food and Beverage

- What type of beverages will we be serving? _____
- Will it be a hosted bar or cash bar? _____
- Will we provide champagne or any other beverage for toasting?

  _____

- What type of food do I see being served at our wedding reception?

  _____

Bridal Couple Departure

- Will there be any special fanfare as we depart? _____
- Where do I see us spending our first night together?_____
- How will we be transported from the wedding reception?_____

Pre-Wedding Events

- Is a "traditional" bachelor/bachelorette party something that we will consider attending, or would it cause conflict? Will we be open to having a destination or joint bachelor/bachelorette party instead? _____

  _____

Wedding Rehearsal

- Will we be holding a wedding dress rehearsal? _____
- Will a rehearsal dinner be a part of our plans? _____
- Do I see it as being casual or formal? _____
- What will be the ideal location in which to hold our rehearsal dinner?

  _____

Wedding Vision Questionnaire

- Who will be included in the rehearsal dinner (e.g., just the wedding party or will out-of-town guests be open to attending as well)? _____

_____

Bride's Attire Considerations

- What style of wedding dress will I be wearing, and will I be buying, borrowing, or renting it? _____

- Will I be wearing a wedding veil? If so, will I be buying, borrowing, or renting it? _____

- Will I be wearing a headpiece? If so, will I be buying, borrowing, or renting it? _____

- What jewelry that I own will I be wearing? _____

- What jewelry will I need to buy or borrow to complete my wedding look? _____

- Will I be having my hair professionally done? _____

- Will I be having my makeup professionally done or purchase any? ____

_____

- Will I be getting a professional manicure and pedicure? _____

- Will I need to buy special bridal shoes for the ceremony? _____

- What special lingerie will I be required to buy? _____

- What will be my something old? _____

- What will be my something new? _____

- What will be my something borrowed? _____

- What will be my something blue? _____

- Will my wedding ring need to be purchased? _____

- Will I be wearing gloves? If so, short or long? _____

- Will I need to purchase a small purse? _____

- Will I need to buy a garter? _____

- Will I be purchasing a special perfume for my wedding day?

_____

Wedding Vision Questionnaire

- Will I need to pull together a mini personal care pouch filled with essential wedding day items for the bride, groom, and wedding party that one of my bridal attendants will carry throughout the day?
  _____

- Will I need a special going-away ensemble? _____
- Will I need to buy special going-away shoes? _____
- Will I need to buy going-away accessories? _____

Groom's Attire Considerations
- Will I be wearing a formal tuxedo, morning suit, or dress suit? ____
- Will I be renting, buying, or do I own my wedding clothing? _____
- Will I be renting, buying, or do I own proper dress shoes? _____
- What personal clothing items will I need to buy? _____
- Will I be purchasing a wedding band? _____
- What grooming aids will I require? _____
- Will I be having any professional grooming services done? _____
- What jewelry do I own that I will I be wearing (e.g., cuff links, tie pin, watch, etc.)? _____
- Will I need to purchase special cologne? _____
- Will I need to buy going-away apparel? _____
- Will I need to buy going-away accessories? _____

Wedding Party Attire Considerations
- Will we be paying—in full or in part—for the wedding party attire, or will they be paying for all their own expenses? _____
- Will being a part of wedding party—if we are not paying all expenses—be a financial hardship for anyone? Are we putting anyone in a tight situation? _____
- Will we be giving gifts to all members of the wedding party?
  _____

Wedding Vision Questionnaire

Honeymoon Considerations
- Will we be going on a honeymoon immediately after the wedding, the next day, or later? _____
- What will be the perfect honeymoon destination for us? _____
_____
- How long will we be away, ideally? _____
- Do we know how much money we need to set aside for our honeymoon and expenses while we are away? _____

Other Wedding Budget Considerations
- Will we be holding any pre-wedding events for out-of-town guests?
_____
- Will we need to budget for bringing in special family members, wedding party, or guests to our wedding who may not be able to attend otherwise? _____
- Do we know if our families will be contributing to our wedding? Will this cause financial hardship for anyone? Are we putting anyone in a tight situation if we accept his or her offer? _____
- If our families are contributing to our wedding costs, do we know what dollars they will be providing (these are the budget parameters we need to be respectful of to ensure that there are no financial hardships incurred)? _____
- If our families are helping us with wedding expenses, will the money be given as a gift for us to use towards our total costs or will it come with concessions that need to be made that could change how we see our wedding day unfolding? _____
_____
- In exchange for family financial assistance, are we prepared to compromise what may be important to us as a couple (if the money given is not strictly a gift to help with wedding costs but comes with certain conditions attached)? _____

Wedding Vision Questionnaire

- What is our personal spending budget? If we are paying for the wedding on our own or paying for all expenses over and above what our families are contributing, what can we afford to spend without putting ourselves in debt or at financial risk? _____
  _____

- Is what we are planning to do financially feasible given our preferred wedding date? _____

License and Legalities

Marriage License

Office Address: _____

Contact Name(s): _____

Contact Number(s): _____

Appointment Date & Time: _____

Cost: _____

Additional Copies: _____

Waiting Period: _____

Requirements

Requirements vary from state to state. For more complete information, visit your county clerk's office.

- Age
- Proof of residency
- Blood tests
- Witnesses for signing application (Maid of Honor and Best Man)
- Proof of citizenship (U.S. or foreign)
- Proof of previous marriage (if applicable)
- Letters of parental consent (minors only, age varies by state)
- Tax information

Notify of Change of Address and/or Name Change

- ❏ Post Office
- ❏ Insurance Policies
- ❏ Driver's License
- ❏ Passport
- ❏ Social Security Card
- ❏ Medical Records
- ❏ Tax Forms
- ❏ Phone Company and Other Utilities

License and Legalities

- ❏ Employee Records
- ❏ Deeds, Mortgages, and Leases
- ❏ Banks and Other Financial Institutions
- ❏ Voter Registration
- ❏ Wills
- ❏ Credit Card Companies
- ❏ Stocks and Investment Funds
- ❏ Schools and Alumni Associations
- ❏ Magazine Subscriptions
- ❏ Mailing Lists
- ❏ Music/Movie Club Memberships
- ❏ Club Memberships (gyms, etc.)
- ❏ Store Memberships (warehouse clubs, etc.)
- ❏ Update Email Address
- ❏ Update Email Contacts
- ❏ Website List Serves

Budget Planning Guide

* Make as many copies as necessary *

Venues

Venues	Estimated Cost	Actual Cost
Site Rental		
Taxes, Service Charges, and Gratuities		
Staffing		
Gratuities		
Setup Costs		
Teardown Costs		
Cleaning		
Insurance		
Permits		

Invitations

Invitations	Estimated Cost	Actual Cost
Save the Date Cards		
Invitations		
RSVP Cards		
Thank-You Cards		
Postage		
Printing		
Calligrapher		
Custom Labels		

Budget Planning Guide

Transportation

	Estimated Cost	Actual Cost
Parking		
Limousines or Motor Coaches		
Parking Permits		
Valet Parking		
Traffic Direction		
Police Escort		

Wedding
Ceremony Arrival

	Estimated Cost	Actual Cost
Coat Check		
Décor		
Rentals (chairs, aisle runner, etc.)		
Music and Entertainment		
Flowers		
Photographer		
Wedding Officiant		
License		

Wedding Reception

	Estimated Cost	Actual Cost
Coat Check		
Food		
Beverage		
Taxes, Service Charges, and Gratuities		
Table décor (table tops, china, crystal, silverware, linens, overlays, runners, napkins, chair covers, draping, floral arrangements, centerpieces, etc.)		
Room Décor		
Rentals (cocktail or cruiser tables, tables, chairs, etc.)		
Music and Entertainment		
Audiovisual Requirements (staging, lighting, and special effects)		
Photographer		
Staffing		
Gratuities		
Print Material (place cards, menus, etc.)		
Wedding Favors		

Suppliers Information Worksheet

Fill in this worksheet and make copies to hand or fax to prospective suppliers. Also check each section below for additional information specific suppliers may need.

- Wedding date _____
- Time and location of ceremony _____ _____
- Time and location of reception _____ _____
- Are floor plans available? _____
- When you will have access to the ceremony venue _____
- When you will have access to the reception venue _____
- What time guests will be arriving and departing _____ _____
- What you envision taking place with regard to timing _____ _____
- When you will have to be out _____
- Do the venues have any restrictions the supplier should know about? _____ _____
- Contact person for ceremony venue _____ _____
- Contact person for reception venue _____ _____
- The number of guests (be sure to include suppliers and the wedding officiant in your count if appropriate for food and beverages, seating, etc.) _____ _____
- Your budget _____
- Colors of ceremony venue _____
- Colors of reception venue _____
- Type and style of meal and beverage service _____ _____

Guest List Worksheet

Name(s):

_____

Address:

_____

_____

_____

Contact Number(s):

_____

Gift Received:

_____

Special Notes/Meals:

_____

❏ Ceremony

❏ Reception

❏ Both

❏ RSVP Rec'd

❏ Gift Rec'd

❏ Thank You Card Sent

Of Guests _____

Table # _____

Name(s):

_____

Address:

_____

_____

_____

Contact Number(s):

_____

Gift Received:

_____

Special Notes/Meals:

_____

❏ Ceremony

❏ Reception

❏ Both

❏ RSVP Rec'd

❏ Gift Rec'd

❏ Thank You Card Sent

Of Guests _____

Table # _____

Guest List Worksheet

Name(s):

_____

Address:

_____

_____

_____

Contact Number(s):

_____

Gift Received:

_____

Special Notes/Meals:

_____

❑ Ceremony

❑ Reception

❑ Both

❑ RSVP Rec'd

❑ Gift Rec'd

❑ Thank You Card Sent

Of Guests _____

Table # _____

Name(s):

_____

Address:

_____

_____

_____

Contact Number(s):

_____

Gift Received:

_____

Special Notes/Meals:

_____

❑ Ceremony

❑ Reception

❑ Both

❑ RSVP Rec'd

❑ Gift Rec'd

❑ Thank You Card Sent

Of Guests _____

Table # _____

Wedding Party Contact Sheet

Wedding Party

Include each person's responsibilities (e.g., matron of honor, best man, etc.), as your point person may not personally know them.

Best Man

Name: _____   Name: _____

Address: _____   Address: _____

_____   _____

Phone (H): _____   Phone (H): _____

Phone (C): _____   Phone (C): _____

Phone (W): _____   Phone (W): _____

Other: _____   Other: _____

_____   _____

Ushers/Groomsmen

Name: _____   Name: _____

Address: _____   Address: _____

_____   _____

Phone (H): _____   Phone (H): _____

Phone (C): _____   Phone (C): _____

Phone (W): _____   Phone (W): _____

Other: _____   Other: _____

_____   _____

Name: _____   Name: _____

Address: _____   Address: _____

_____   _____

Phone (H): _____   Phone (H): _____

Phone (C): _____   Phone (C): _____

Phone (W): _____   Phone (W): _____

Other: _____   Other: _____

_____   _____

Wedding Party Contact Sheet

Maid/Matron of Honor

Name: _____   Name: _____

Address: _____   Address: _____

_____   _____

Phone (H): _____   Phone (H): _____

Phone (C): _____   Phone (C): _____

Phone (W): _____   Phone (W): _____

Other: _____   Other: _____

_____   _____

Bridesmaids

Name: _____   Name: _____

Address: _____   Address: _____

_____   _____

Phone (H): _____   Phone (H): _____

Phone (C): _____   Phone (C): _____

Phone (W): _____   Phone (W): _____

Other: _____   Other: _____

_____   _____

Name: _____   Name: _____

Address: _____   Address: _____

_____   _____

Phone (H): _____   Phone (H): _____

Phone (C): _____   Phone (C): _____

Phone (W): _____   Phone (W): _____

Other: _____   Other: _____

_____   _____

Wedding Party Contact Sheet

Bride's Parents

Name: _____   Name: _____

Address: _____   Address: _____

_____   _____

Phone (H): _____   Phone (H): _____

Phone (C): _____   Phone (C): _____

Phone (W): _____   Phone (W): _____

Other: _____   Other: _____

_____   _____

Groom's Parents

Name: _____   Name: _____

Address: _____   Address: _____

_____   _____

Phone (H): _____   Phone (H): _____

Phone (C): _____   Phone (C): _____

Phone (W): _____   Phone (W): _____

Other: _____   Other: _____

_____   _____

Officiant

Name: _____   Name: _____

Address: _____   Address: _____

_____   _____

Phone (H): _____   Phone (H): _____

Phone (C): _____   Phone (C): _____

Phone (W): _____   Phone (W): _____

Other: _____   Other: _____

_____   _____

Wedding Party Contact Sheet

Wedding Team

List everyone who will be helping out with setup, move-in, rehearsal, wedding day, teardown, and move-out.

Name: _____   Name: _____
Address: _____   Address: _____
_____   _____
Phone (H): _____   Phone (H): _____
Phone (C): _____   Phone (C): _____
Phone (W): _____   Phone (W): _____
Other: _____   Other: _____

Name: _____   Name: _____
Address: _____   Address: _____
_____   _____
Phone (H): _____   Phone (H): _____
Phone (C): _____   Phone (C): _____
Phone (W): _____   Phone (W): _____
Other: _____   Other: _____

Name: _____   Name: _____
Address: _____   Address: _____
_____   _____
Phone (H): _____   Phone (H): _____
Phone (C): _____   Phone (C): _____
Phone (W): _____   Phone (W): _____
Other: _____   Other: _____

Name: _____   Name: _____
Address: _____   Address: _____
_____   _____
Phone (H): _____   Phone (H): _____
Phone (C): _____   Phone (C): _____
Phone (W): _____   Phone (W): _____
Other: _____   Other: _____

Final Guest Seating Chart

R=Reception (Light Food & Beverages Pre-Meal)

M=Meal (Sit-Down Service Following Reception)

# Guests R	# Guests M	# Tables of 6	# Tables of 8	# Tables of 10	# Head Table
_____	_____	_____	_____	_____	_____

Table # _____

1. _____
2. _____
3. _____
4. _____
5. _____
6. _____
7. _____
8. _____
9. _____
10. _____

Special Notes: _____

_____

Table # _____

1. _____
2. _____
3. _____
4. _____
5. _____
6. _____
7. _____
8. _____
9. _____
10. _____

Special Notes: _____

_____

Table # _____

1. _____
2. _____
3. _____
4. _____
5. _____
6. _____
7. _____
8. _____
9. _____
10. _____

Special Notes: _____

_____

Table # _____

1. _____
2. _____
3. _____
4. _____
5. _____
6. _____
7. _____
8. _____
9. _____
10. _____

Special Notes: _____

_____

Final Guest Seating Chart

Table # _____

1. _____
2. _____
3. _____
4. _____
5. _____
6. _____
7. _____
8. _____
9. _____
10. _____

Special Notes: _____

_____

Table # _____

1. _____
2. _____
3. _____
4. _____
5. _____
6. _____
7. _____
8. _____
9. _____
10. _____

Special Notes: _____

_____

Table # _____

1. _____
2. _____
3. _____
4. _____
5. _____
6. _____
7. _____
8. _____
9. _____
10. _____

Special Notes: _____

_____

Table # _____

1. _____
2. _____
3. _____
4. _____
5. _____
6. _____
7. _____
8. _____
9. _____
10. _____

Special Notes: _____

_____

About the Author

~

Judy Allen is a professional event planner, life planning, and lifestyle expert. Author of *Your Stress Free Wedding Planner*, she has created, produced, and flawlessly executed successful corporate, social, and celebrity special events with up to two thousand guests in more than thirty countries. As one of the leading authorities on event planning, she is the author of eight professional bestselling books on the subject, and has written an "Entertaining Ideas" column for the *New York Post's* Page Six. Allen currently has two lifestyle television shows under development and will be releasing a new consumer lifestyle book series in 2008 based on the two television series.